I'll Do It!

Written by Brian Moses

Illustrated by Mike Gordon

sundance

A Haights Cross Communications Company

Kids Corner Books

KID-TO-KID BOOKS

I Feel Angry	I Feel Bored	I Feel Bullied	Excuse Me!
I Feel Happy	I Feel Jealous	I Feel Frightened	I Don't Care!
I Feel Lonely	I Feel Shy	I Feel Sad	I'll Do It!
It's Not Fair	I Feel Worried	Why Wash?	It Wasn't Me!

LITERACY STORIES

Dogs Can't Read
Mice Can't Write
Spiders Can't Spell
Cats Can't Count

This edition published
in North America by
Sundance Publishing
P.O. Box 1326
234 Taylor Street
Littleton, MA 01460

First published in 1997 by Wayland Publishers Limited
Copyright © 1997 Wayland Publishers Limited

ISBN 0-7608-3923-9

Printed in Canada

In the corner today,
we're talking about

being responsible.

This way to Kids Corner

3

I try to be responsible.
I clean my room.
I pick up my toys.

And I hardly ever
just cram stuff in my closet
so that I can go outside to play.

I'm so responsible
that I almost never
have to be told

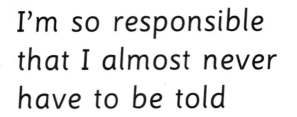

to comb my own hair

or brush my own teeth—

6

except when I forget.

I'm really responsible around the house when I know company is coming.

I make my bed,

and I water the plants.

And I'd never dream
of hiding dirty socks
in my trash can—
except in an emergency.

Even when it's not fun,
I baby-sit my little brother.

No, Larry, I don't think
he should be eating
the cat's dinner.

11

I feel really grown-up
when I take care of other people.

And I try to think of others first.

I try not to forget to feed my dog
and play with her
and clean up after her.

But taking care of my hamster
is a little tricky.
He thinks Mom's new hairdo
is a playground.

I take care of things
so they don't get ruined.

I put my books back on the shelves,
except when I want
to use them
all at once.

And I put my videos back in their cases.

One time I didn't,
and the dog thought
she'd found a new toy . . .

I try to remember to be very careful around the computer.

But I don't think
my hamster has learned that rule yet!

I try to act grown-up
when we go shopping.

And I try to help by picking out what we're having for dessert.

Sometimes being responsible means being a hero and saving the day.

But sometimes,
even a hero needs help.

I'm really having trouble carrying all this stuff. Do you think you could carry this CD home for me?

I'm getting pretty good at
not forgetting things.

I'd be pretty sad
if I left my favorite toy behind—
he'd be sad, too.

And it is pretty hard to play soccer when my uniform is at the bottom of the Lost and Found box.

I've figured out that
when I take care of things, people notice.
Then they trust me to do things for them.
I get to do neat things like—

taking packages
to the office,

putting away
library books,

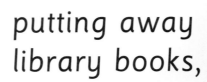

sharpening pencils,

 and feeding Jaws,
our class fish.

27

Sometimes I help the little kids get dressed, or I shovel Grandma's walkway.

I feel good about myself when I help.

I know I'd get a high score for responsibility.

How high would your score be?

A REALLY
RESPONSIBLE
PERSON

YOU'VE
ALMOST
MADE IT

QUITE
RESPONSIBLE

TRYING
HARDER

NOT
VERY
RESPONSIBLE

Things to Do in the Kids Corner

Use a familiar tune and make up words to a song about being responsible. Find a friend to sing your song with you. Tape-record the song, and then play it for the class.

Trace one of your hands on a large, blank piece of paper. Around the tracing, write different ways you use your hands to help yourself and others.

How many words can you make using only the letters in *responsibility*? Make a list and have a friend do the same. Compare your lists.

teddy

my mom

Other Books to Read

A Busy Year, by Leo Lionni (Alfred A. Knopf, Inc., 1992). Willie and Winnie mouse learn about respecting trees when they befriend a talking tree. Through the year, the mice learn from the tree how to care for all trees. *24 pages*

The Day That Henry Cleaned His Room, by Sarah Wilson (Simon & Schuster Inc., 1990). It is quite an event when Henry cleans his room after a whole year. Scientists, reporters, and the army come to witness the interesting things Henry has been keeping in his room all this time. Henry finds out that having a clean room is hard work. *30 pages*

Frank and Ernest, by Alexandra Day (Scholastic, Inc., 1988). Do-gooders Frank and Ernest run a diner while the owner is away. This duo find out about responsibility and cooperation as they serve the customers just as the owner would. *36 pages*

Getting Ready for School, by Peter and Sheryl Sloan (a Sundance *Little Red Reader*, 1996). Children feel responsible when they see that the girl in the story does the same things that they do to get ready for school in the morning. *8 pages*

Fred Fixes a Faucet, by Pat Edwards (a Sundance *Popcorn* book, 1999). Instead of calling a plumber right away, Fred the pig takes on the responsibility of fixing a broken faucet by himself. Read about the mess that Fred makes. *24 pages*